Live Better reiki

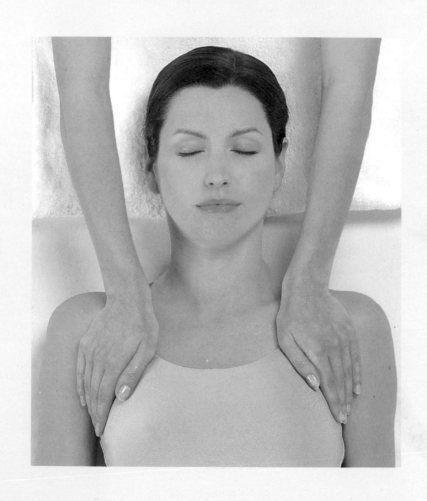

Live Better reiki

exercises for healing and balance

Sandi Leir-Shuffrey

DUNCAN BAIRD PUBLISHERS

LONDON

Live Better: reiki
Sandi Leir-Shuffrey

**To Will Kay for making it, and to Cele Smith –
may Reiki help to lead you home.**

First published in the United Kingdom and Ireland
in 2005 by
Duncan Baird Publishers Ltd
Sixth Floor
Castle House
75–76 Wells Street
London W1T 3QH

Conceived, created and designed by Duncan Baird
Publishers Ltd
Copyright © Duncan Baird Publishers 2005
Text copyright © Sandi Leir-Shuffrey 2005
Commissioned artwork copyright © Duncan Baird
Publishers 2005
Commissioned photography copyright © Duncan Baird
Publishers 2005
For copyright of agency photographs see p.128, which is to
be regarded as an extension of this copyright.

Managing Designer: Manisha Patel
Designer: Allan Sommerville
Managing Editor: Julia Charles
Editor: Ingrid Court-Jones
Picture Research: Julia Ruxton
Commissioned Photography: Matthew Ward

British Library Cataloguing-in-Publication Data:
A CIP record for this book is available from the
British Library.

ISBN-10: 1-84483-094-2
ISBN-13: 9-781844-830947

10 9 8 7 6 5 4 3 2 1

Typeset in Filosofia and Son Kern
Colour reproduction by Scanhouse, Malaysia
Printed by Imago Thailand

Publisher's note
Before following any advice or practice suggested in
this book, it is recommended that you consult your
doctor as to its suitability, especially if you suffer
from any health problems or special conditions.
The publishers, author and photographers cannot
accept any responsibility for any injuries or damage
incurred as a result of following the exercises in this
book, or of using any of the therapeutic techniques
described or mentioned here.

contents

INTRODUCTION

Reiki hands-on healing is one of the fastest growing therapies, not only in clinics but also in the home. The simple, practical application of Reiki makes it very appealing to many people who struggle to cope with the hectic, stressful lifestyles of the modern Western world. Reiki is learnt by nurses, doctors, complementary therapists, beauty therapists, and carers who not only offer it to their patients, but also benefit from applying the treatment to themselves for the release of tension and the prevention of stress. However, Reiki is not the exclusive preserve of therapists and practitioners. Anyone can learn it and improve their well-being.

Stress is a fact of life. It cannot be avoided, but it *can* be harnessed and dealt with in a more creative and beneficial way. By giving the mind respite from its incessant chatter and allowing the body to be still long enough to find deep relaxation, Reiki allows us to become calmer and see the way forward with more clarity. Having been a Reiki Master, teacher and practitioner since 1989, I have often seen first-hand the transformations that happen when individuals find inner stillness and calm through Reiki. The experience of healing allows people to regain lost vitality and to reassess their lives.

It is common for people to feel more integrated during and after a Reiki treatment. Too many years of disintegration through the burden of stress can eventually cause physical tension, emotional pain, mental instability, neurosis and all manner of illnesses. It has been shown that many medical conditions improve once the patient learns to relax and becomes more aware of changes that need to be made to their habits. The way in which we talk to ourselves in our head has to be rebalanced if change is to become permanent and happiness is to be restored as our natural state of being.

In Chapter 1 of this book you will learn about the history and background of Reiki, and how the healing works. In Chapter 2 you will be taken position-by-position through a typical treatment, so that you can understand what it might feel like to have Reiki and appreciate the ongoing positive effects that Reiki has, not only on the body, but also on the mind, the emotions and the spirit.

In Chapter 3 you will discover how to practise Reiki on yourself so that you can become self-empowered by its gift of healing. You will then be able to administer self-help on a day-to-day basis to relieve stress and increase your happiness and well-being. You will also find out how you can reach out to treat your family, friends (and even the dog!), through Reiki therapy.

In Chapter 4 you will explore how Reiki can change your consciousness. You will also find guidance if you wish to practise Reiki professionally, whether by itself or in addition to other therapies, and you will learn about further training.

Reiki is a non-invasive healing treatment that can be safely applied to any condition because you are treating the person rather than the condition – when the person starts to feel better within themselves, their condition also begins to improve. As an experienced practitioner, I would like to invite you to learn to live better through practising Reiki – you won't be disappointed!

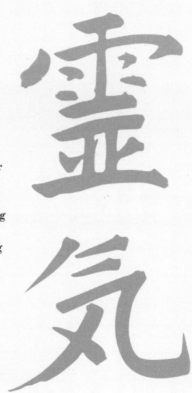

This is the Japanese "kanji" or character for the word "reiki". It is made up of two parts: the top is "rei" meaning "universal", and the bottom is "ki" meaning "life force".

what is reiki?

As we have seen, the word "reiki" is Japanese, and is made up from two words: "rei", meaning "universal", and "ki" meaning "life force". It is the energy that creates everything around and within us. Reiki is an ancient, simple and practical technique for deep relaxation and hands-on healing. Through Reiki empowerment and training we can make a direct connection to the unlimited supply of universal energy around us. We can then access and draw it in by applying our hands to ourselves or to another person. Reiki not only rebalances the physical body, but also clears the mind, calms the emotions and reawakens our connection with our spirituality. It is the perfect tool to use on ourselves to combat day-to-day stress, as it aids relaxation and promotes well-being.

When you give Reiki to another person, your hands hold their body still while the energy flows in unhindered *through* you (not *from* you) and then enters the recipient. This means that you do not give away any of your own precious energy in the process.

Reiki is hard to describe in words as it is essentially an experience — you will understand it fully when you feel it yourself. You may experience a warm tingling feeling, a sense of well-being or even relief from physical, mental or emotional pain. Or you may simply have a new sense of the life force within you.

THE ORIGINS AND HISTORY OF REIKI

Dr Mikao Usui, a Japanese Buddhist monk, put Reiki into its current form at the end of the nineteenth century. After extensive research into ancient scriptures, he spent 21 days sitting on a holy mountain, fasting and meditating on sacred symbols and mantras which he had found in the Buddhist texts. It is said that on the twenty-first day he saw each symbol in turn in his mind, surrounded by a brilliant golden light. When he stood up he realized that he had changed. Usui soon discovered that if he laid his hands on someone who was in pain, they would rapidly feel better.

He then decided that he should pass on his skills and so created the current form of teaching and practice. He called this original form Usui Shiki Reiki Ryoho — the Usui System of Healing with Universal Energy. Usui found that by using the symbols in a certain way he could transmit the empowerment of energy to others so that they too could start healing. After spending several years helping poor people in Kyoto, he noticed that they often failed to take advantage of their newfound well-being. Usui then concluded that in order to be effectively healed, receivers of Reiki needed to have a sincere desire to be helped. He moved to a clinic in Tokyo where he formed a partnership with Dr Chujuro Hayashi, a medical doctor who was keen to learn Reiki. Usui taught Hayashi how to access Reiki and together they created the basis for all Reiki forms that have since followed.

When Usui allowed Hayashi to teach, he founded the lineage of Reiki Masters. The lineage of every teaching Master should be traceable back to Usui. My own is: Usui, Hayashi, Hawayo Takata, Wanja Twan, Martha Sylvester and, finally, me. I learnt Reiki in 1988 and set up my own school in 1989 when I became a Master. My principles are to honour the simplicity of Usui Shiki Reiki Ryoho and to keep it accessible to everyday people.

Today Reiki has evolved into many different forms, most of which have incorporated extra techniques and information so that they are quite different from Usui's original form. For this reason, it is important to choose both your therapist and your teacher wisely (see p.32).

THE FOUR DEGREES OF REIKI

Usui Shiki Reiki Ryoho is taught by a Master who has a short lineage (no more than seven masters) back to Usui. Learning Reiki is divided into four degrees or stages, with intervals in between each course to allow the student to gain an understanding of what they have already learned before going further. Many people are quite content simply to do Reiki First Degree, while others feel the need to deepen their understanding and practice by progressing to Reiki Second Degree and beyond to the Master's Levels. It is a matter of personal choice and commitment.

I shall describe the degrees more fully in Chapter 4, but here is a summary.

Reiki First Degree

This is for anyone who wants to understand Reiki and activate their ability to heal themselves, the members of their family and their friends, including babies, children and animals.

Reiki Second Degree

This is for anyone who has completed Reiki First Degree who wishes to deepen their Reiki practice and understanding, whether for self-treatment or for healing family and friends. It includes learning how to heal from a distance. This level is a pre-requisite for practitioners.

Reiki Master's Level 1

This level is for anyone wishing to work toward finding spiritual enlightenment and gaining personal mastery. If you decide to progress to this level, strong commitment to regular self-treatment will lead you to a deeper understanding of universal energy and the meaning of consciousness.

Reiki Master's Level 2 – Teacher

This level is for experienced practitioners who have completed the other levels and now wish to teach Reiki to others. Training for this level requires great dedication as it can take several years. Some Masters take on students for mastership by invitation only.

A journey of a thousand miles must
begin with a single step.

LAO-TZU

(604—531BCE)

We shape clay into a pot, but it is the emptiness
inside that holds whatever we want.

LAO-TZU

(604—531BCE)

THE FIVE REIKI PRECEPTS

The following precepts were taught by Dr Mikao Usui. They can be used for contemplation and to help change common sources of negativity into positive affirmations. If you focus on these phrases daily, your attitude toward both yourself and the world around you will change for the better.

Turn anger into peace

Anger is a condensed form of energy and a natural emotion that we should never suppress. However, as stored anger can cause all manner of illnesses, including heart conditions, high blood pressure, digestive disorders and depression, you should allow yourself to express it and then transform it quickly into a less harmful emotion. When you are feeling angry sit still in a quiet place and focus on your breathing. Then repeat the first precept below in your mind as an affirmation, contemplating its meaning:

Just for today I am at peace.

Turn worry into clarity

Worry is a mental preoccupation with thoughts about something that may happen in the future, based on your experience of the past and fed with fear. Long-term worry and anxiety can cause mental stress, neurosis, panic attacks, low self-esteem and deep unhappiness. When you find yourself worrying, sit still in a quiet place and focus on your breathing. Then repeat the second precept below in your mind as an affirmation, contemplating its meaning:

Just for today my mind is at rest.

A statement of honesty

Dishonesty causes secrets and lies which, in turn, create inner tension and illness. If you know that the third precept, below, is true of your life, then take time to humbly praise yourself. However, if it is not true, sit in a quiet place, repeat this affirmation and contemplate the changes you need to make:

I earn my living honestly and do no harm to anyone, to anything or to the environment.

A statement of honour

Honour is based on respect. It should not involve our likes or dislikes. We must respect that each person lives their own journey in their own reality. Dishonour is based on fear and anger, which we need to deal with so that we remain in good health. Actively honour your family, friends and those around you for they are an intricate part of what makes you unique. Sit in a quiet place and repeat the fourth precept below in your mind as an affirmation, contemplating its meaning:

I honour my parents, elders, teachers, children, friends and myself.

An attitude of gratitude

Gratitude teaches us the art of giving rather than receiving. Receiving has its place when it allows another person the pleasure of giving. It is an acknowledgment of the gift of energy that has been directed to you. An attitude of gratitude will bring abundance. Sit in your quiet place, and repeat the fifth precept in your mind as an affirmation, contemplating its meaning:

I give thanks to every living thing and for every situation whatever form it may take, for within it is contained my growth and understanding.

Coping with change: fear versus love

Day-to-day stress builds up to cause tension in our bodies and changes in both our moods and reactions. As we learn and grow, we encounter a variety of experiences from joyous, happy and pleasant, through to difficult, conflicting and even traumatic. For example, if we increase our workload and take on more and more responsibilities, it is often the case that the tension in our bodies becomes tighter and deeper. However, we cannot hide away and avoid the difficulties in life as they are part of what makes us unique.

Our personal history is given to us to help us to develop. If our experiences in early life make us fearful and angry, this will affect our self-esteem, our response to injustice and our feelings of security. We may know that we need to change, but our fears may stop us from making those changes.

If you contemplate the precepts and reassess your attitude to life and the people in it, you can begin to transform the energy of anger, frustration, hurt and fear into the energy of calm, ease, enjoyment and love. If you do nothing and continue to be frenetic and tense, you will only prolong your negative feelings. Through self-empowerment you can begin to awaken to your own reality and see from your own true perspective.

Love cannot dwell where fear resides and likewise fear cannot dwell where love resides. Love and peace are not missing from your life. Love and peace are there within you to feel. They are just masked by the build-up of all those other negative feelings and by the incessant chatter in your head. Love, joy and happiness are states of being. By being quiet and still, by receiving a Reiki treatment or simply by enjoying the present moment, you can allow some of your anger and frustration to dissipate. And by contemplating the qualities you would like to regain in your life, you begin to activate them and attract them. If you wish to feel more love, all you have to do is become still and invite love in.

ILLNESS VERSUS HEALTH

Illnesses develop when we ignore our bodies' needs. When an illness occurs in our body, this means that our energy field has been out of balance for a long time. If we ignore the signs, they will only get worse. However, if we reconsider our way of life and begin to change our words, our actions and our deeds, a shift takes place – as our consciousness evolves and our knowledge grows, so our energy field starts to create a new being and a new body. This concept may seem initially hard to grasp, yet it works very simply.

The electromagnetic energy field (also known as the aura) of a healthy, happy person expands many feet beyond their body. Conversely, the energy field of a person suffering from stress or illness remains close to their body and has a dense, foggy appearance. In anyone who smokes, drinks alcohol excessively or abuses other substances, this fog is thick and dull. When our energy field is tight and close, there is only so much stress that we can handle before we become overloaded. If this happens our energy implodes and our body's chemistry changes, making us more susceptible to illness.

There are seven major energy centres, known as "chakras", in the body's electromagnetic system. These areas vibrate in concentrated spirals and hold together the anatomy and physiology of the body. They are located at each curve of the spine and vibrate through and beyond the front and back of the physical body.

The Root Chakra is found at the base of the spine around the coccyx, and vibrates at the colour frequency of red. The Sacral Chakra is located at the lower end of the spine, about three fingers below the navel. It vibrates at the colour frequency of orange. The Solar Plexus Chakra is based at the diaphragm and vibrates at the colour frequency of yellow. The Heart Chakra is located in the centre of the chest and in the thymus gland, vibrating at the colour frequency of green. The Throat Chakra is sited at the throat, in the thyroid gland, and vibrates at the colour frequency of blue. The Third Eye Chakra is between the eyebrows, in the pituitary gland, and vibrates at the colour frequency of violet.

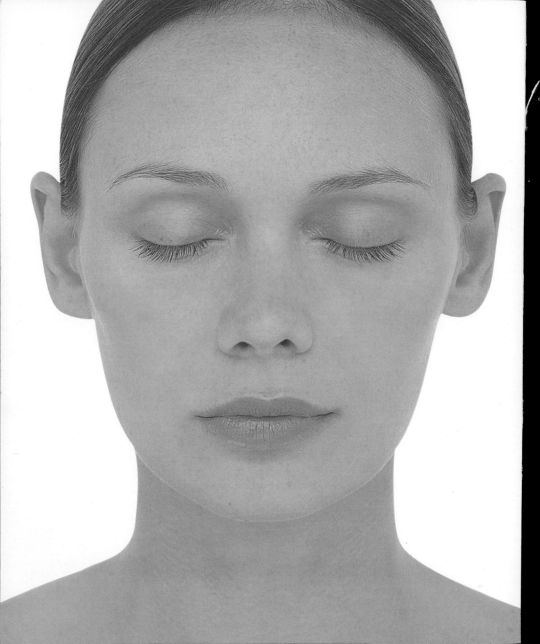

Finally, the Crown Chakra is found at the top of the head, where our skulls were open when we were babies. It spins through the pineal gland and vibrates at the colour frequency of white light. These energy centres can be put out of balance through shock, trauma, despair or any other negative emotion. The Reiki treatment is an effective way to help them to realign.

During a Reiki treatment, the practitioner gathers up and holds still the receiver's energy field. It is then allowed to expand naturally as their body relaxes. The receiver starts to feel better as their mental tension is released. They may also feel a tingling sensation, like bubbles of lemonade fizzing all over their body, as balance is restored. When the treatment is over, typically the receiver's facial lines seem less pronounced, healthy colour has returned to their cheeks and their eyes look brighter. Often they have increased flexibility in their neck and joints, too.

By learning how to treat ourselves, we can keep our energy in balance and become happier as we equip ourselves to deal creatively with stress and difficulties.

WHY HAVE REIKI THERAPY?

It is my belief that people come for Reiki therapy because they need to feel nurtured. They are attracted to Reiki, perhaps unconsciously, because imbalances or blockages in their energy field are manifesting themselves physically or mentally, and they need to be healed. There is something about the word "healing" that is comforting and non-judgmental. Reiki provides a safe haven away from the world, a place where calm and stillness can once again be felt.

Many physical conditions arise as a result of long-term stress or poor attention to diet. And many of us take medication for a variety of illnesses because we don't give ourselves time to reflect on the alternatives. While prescribed drugs can provide a quick-fix solution, they cannot solve the long-term problem of unhappiness. I see many clients who take antidepressants instead of taking time out to relax and be healed from the inside. Over time Reiki treatment can create profound positive changes in body, mind and spirit.

What conditions can Reiki treat?

Reiki can treat most illnesses and conditions under the majority of circumstances as it is non-invasive. It is safe to use on anyone of any age, including babies, children and the elderly. Reiki can also be used on animals, and even for distance-healing.

Specific problems that Reiki can treat include heart conditions, high blood pressure, irritable bowel syndrome, M.E., ulcers, migraines and neck and back pain, as well as more general symptoms, such as tiredness and depression. It can aid the healing of injuries and broken bones and it can help to rebalance hormones and lessen the discomforts of pregnancy.

Reiki works on all levels and can be useful in the treatment of predominantly mental conditions, such as anxiety, phobias and insomnia. It can also help emotional conditions such as unhappiness, grief, loneliness and low self-esteem.

And finally, Reiki can also help us to find clarity of direction in terms of our spirituality, our vocation in life and our relationships.

REIKI FOR CARERS

It is always a great pleasure to teach Reiki to people who work looking after others, whether in an institution such as a hospital or a clinic, or as a carer of a disabled, elderly or sick person at home. When people are institutionalized because of illness or disability, they can feel frightened and literally "out of touch". Reiki brings back that touch and with it a sense of connection and belonging as a human being. Reiki has not yet been integrated into many hospitals as a separate therapy but there are a growing number of nurses, physiotherapists, occupational therapists and other carers who can offer Reiki as an additional aid to the physical healing process.

Chronic illness leaves people feeling isolated and at the mercy of others. But when they feel supported, they begin to feel safe. The terminally ill cannot avoid their fate, yet Reiki offers them a way of coming to terms and accepting what is happening to them. In fact, it is reported by Reiki volunteers who visit hospices on a regular basis that patients who undergo regular Reiki treatments enjoy a better quality of life and often live longer than those who do not.

Contraindications

There are very few people for whom Reiki is not recommended. One group is people who have had organ transplants. The other is those with severe mental illness, who may be unable to take responsibility for their actions. That is not to say that Reiki must be ruled out entirely in these cases, but that it should only be undertaken by an experienced therapist who has specific training in these areas.

Reiki should never be given to anyone with a contagious or infectious disease as this could jeopardise the health of the therapist and their other clients. In such cases, distance-healing is more appropriate. Similarly, the therapist should never treat anyone while he or she has an infectious or contagious condition or if he or she is very tired. Recent wounds or sensitive skin should be given Reiki with the hands an inch or so above the body to avoid discomfort.

CHOOSING A THERAPIST

If you wish to have ongoing sessions of Reiki to boost your immune system and to prevent the build-up of stress, it is absolutely vital to choose a therapist with whom you feel comfortable, safe and supported. It is also important that your therapist has sufficient training and experience – any Reiki practitioner should have First and Second Degree Reiki, be registered with one or more of the relevant associations and be fully insured.

There are several associations and regulatory bodies that govern complementary therapies, holding registers of practitioners and advising on their qualifications. Some even specify minimum standards for Reiki training. Many practitioners may be qualified in more than one therapy and might offer other types of treatment separately, for example, Deep Body-Balancing or Emotional Therapy. I normally recommend that clients receive *only* Reiki during a treatment. However, sometimes it can be appropriate to undergo other therapies within the same session (see p.118).

Chapter Two

the reiki treatment

Touch is an unspoken form of communication that allows love to pass from one person to another. From the moment we are born we yearn for the reassurance of our mother's touch. Then, throughout our formative years, we rely on the constant love and support of our family and friends, which is often expressed through touch. Research has shown that people who are rarely touched, especially when they are children, are more likely to suffer from social disorders, mental illness and depression as adults.

It is hardly surprising then that touch is a most valuable tool for healing. When we receive Reiki we allow another person – often a complete stranger – to touch us. We let them into our space and give them our trust; we invite them to hold us still while we heal from the inside. The therapist keeps their hands very still, neither prodding nor massaging us. Many people liken the warmth and comfort they receive from the Reiki experience to being held in their mother's arms again. In this secure state we can finally let go of all tensions and allow ourselves to relax deeply.

In this chapter we explore the importance of time out and rest, and learn what to expect in a typical Reiki treatment. Each Reiki hand position is then depicted, accompanied by a brief explanation of the particular benefits that it will bring.

THE IMPORTANCE OF TIME-OUT

Most of us have favourite ways in which we wind down and relax. Some of us might like to go for a walk or listen to music, while others prefer to watch television, read a book or take an aerobics class. These are all good ways to release stress or promote health, but they all contain an element of entertainment – the mind switches from being entertained by stressful thoughts to being entertained by an alternative activity.

By contrast, when you receive a Reiki treatment your mind is allowed to rest completely. Only in stillness and silence can we look inward and begin to feel our spirit. It is therefore important not to be tempted to play relaxation tapes or burn fragrances during a treatment. Music, smell and even bright light keep the mind and the senses distracted.

Even if we cannot have Reiki every day, we should all spend some time daily when we do absolutely nothing. Try to sit still and empty your mind. See how quickly thoughts intrude and you find yourself thinking about having a cup of tea, wondering what time it is or making a mental list of things you need to do. Don't let this put you off. Doing nothing is actually very difficult and you will need to practise! Start with five minutes' time out per day and gradually build up to fifteen. No matter how busy you are, put aside a short period in which to stop and empty your mind. Even a few minutes a day is better than any amount of good intentions.

You will need to find a quiet place in which to spend your time-out. Choose somewhere peaceful — perhaps your bedroom or a conservatory. Of course, you don't have to stay inside. If you are lucky enough to live in the countryside or near a park, find a quiet spot outside where you can sit and contemplate. Before you start, be sure to smell the earth and the leaves, touch the grass, listen to the birds singing and feel the breeze on your face. Look up at the sky and wonder at the magnificence of being a part of it all. Drink in the beauty of nature and feel joy returning. Then focus inward. Time-out amid a calming green landscape feeds the heart, especially as the colour vibration of the heart chakra is green.

THE IMPORTANCE OF REST

Rest is another essential part of well-being, While time-out lets us focus on stopping our minds, rest allows us to still our bodies and give them time to recharge. A good time to rest would be after time-out.

Lying down is probably the ideal position in which to rest. If we fall asleep that's fine, but sometimes sleep can be filled with agitation and stimulating dreams, so that it is not necessarily restful. In any case, we should all take rest in addition to the sleep we have at night.

We can rest consciously. One of the best ways is through relaxation and deep breathing. Try lying still and just monitoring your breath. Keep your breathing gentle and even, and then gradually slow it down and deepen it. Your body will start to relax and a lot of tension will be released.

After a Reiki treatment I leave my clients to rest for a few minutes without touching them. During this time they can feel the benefit of the treatment yet realize that it is not coming from me – the change is within them.

WHAT TO EXPECT FROM A TREATMENT

When you go for a Reiki treatment with a qualified practitioner, you might be asked to lie down on a therapy couch (which has a hole for your face when you lie on your front). This helps you to keep your neck straight and your shoulder muscles relaxed.

The practitioner will begin by taking your details and a brief medical history. All information given is held in the strictest confidence. You remove your shoes, jewelry and glasses, but remain fully clothed.

The treatment will start with you lying on your back, with pillows under your knees and head for comfort. The therapist will place their hands in various positions on your body as they work down from your head to your feet. They will hold each position for about two minutes. No movement takes place. You will then be asked to turn onto your front. The therapist will finish holding the soles of your feet. By this time you will have benefitted from about 50 minutes of stillness and silence. To bring you back to the outside world the therapist will gently squeeze and flick your back and limbs. They will then leave you on your own for a few minutes to rest and reflect on your experience of the treatment. When they return they will ask you to sit up and give you a glass of water to drink. This prevents dehydration and helps to flush out toxins as they continue to be released into your bloodstream after the session.

How will you feel after the treatment? Everyone reacts diffently, but many people feel lighter, calmer and deeply relaxed. You may feel very energetic, or very tired. But however you feel, begin the process of listening to your body. You will need to drink water frequently during the next 24 hours as an after-effect of the treatment is that you continue to draw in energy for at least this amount of time. You may also notice that your attitude toward people around you, and even toward yourself, changes.

One Reiki treatment can be very therapeutic, but you might need several if long-term changes are to be made. The answer to "How many treatments will I need?" is "Listen, and your body will tell you."

THE HAND POSITIONS

The eyes

Here, the therapist places their hands lightly over your eyes, their thumbs down the middle of your forehead. This position helps to rejuvenate tired eyes and is useful if you spend a lot of time driving or looking at a computer screen. It also quietens the mind and lessens anxiety.

The top of the head

In this position the therapist gently cups your head and applies energy to both sides of your brain, stilling your mind. As we all tend to overuse one side of our brain, this position helps to rebalance the brain and also encourages the integration of thought. It is useful to combat stress, anxiety and hyperactivity, as well as to improve memory and help with learning difficulties.

The jaws and face

In this soothing position the therapist gently cups the jawline, helping to release any pent-up anger that is stored in the jaw joint. The jaw may be especially tense in people who grind their teeth at night. From this position energy also passes into the gums and teeth. As your facial muscles relax, any lines and wrinkles will lessen and your face will take on a youthful glow.

The back of the head

Here, the therapist cups your head with their fingers resting in the ridge of the skull. This position helps to relieve any build-up of tension in the head and the neck. It is particularly good for people who suffer from headaches, migraines or eyestrain. The position of the hands continues to hold the mind still and begins to promote a sense of peace.

The ears

By cupping your ears in this position, the therapist turns the outward projection of sound and the skill of listening inward. This position can relieve ear infections, especially in children. Also, after long-term treatment, some people report that their hearing has improved. When energy blockages are removed here you are better equipped to hear the real meaning behind words.

The throat

In this position the therapist gently rests their hands on your chin, slightly fanning out their fingers without touching your neck or throat. This position helps to treat colds, throat infections and thyroid conditions. Because it focuses on the throat, balancing the energy in this region can also bring about an improvement in your oral communication skills.

The heart

In this position the therapist's hands form a "V" in the centre of your upper chest. This position is used to address physical conditions, such as heart and lung problems and breathing difficulties, as well as to heal emotional pain, such as loss, grief and loneliness. After treatment on the heart area, many people find that their aggression is transformed into assertiveness.

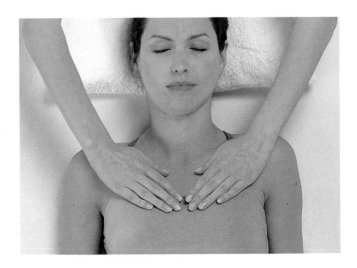

The expanded chest

Here, the therapist places their hands over the top of your chest and armpits, drawing energy down your arms and into the lymphatic system. It is one of the most gentle and supportive positions – often likened to being held in your mother's arms. Many people suffer from tension in their shoulders and upper back because they try to protect their heart by pulling in their front.

The left ribs

Here, the therapist places their hands side by side on your torso, covering the lower area of your lungs and the organs in your upper abdomen, including the spleen, which is said to be the seat of boredom. This position helps with breathing by releasing the muscles in the chest. It also aids digestion and elimination by stimulating the stomach.

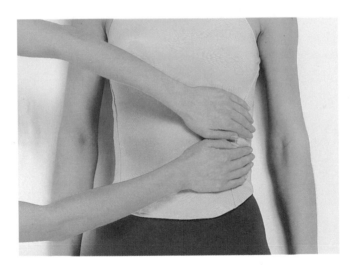

The right ribs

The therapist again places their hands side by side on your torso, but this time on the right side of your body where they cover the liver, which is said to be the seat of anger. Again, this helps to release the breath and chest muscles. As this position also covers the diaphragm, don't be surprised if you find yourself sighing deeply as tension is released and your breathing rhythm changes.

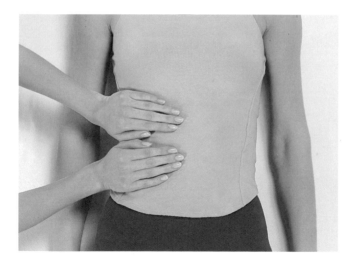

The waist

The therapist places their hands one in front of the other across your waist. This position calms all digestive and nervous disorders. It stimulates the bowels and aids elimination in cases of constipation, as well as reducing irritation and inflammation caused by loose bowels. This is the area of emotion, and treatment here helps us to find a balance between holding on and letting go.

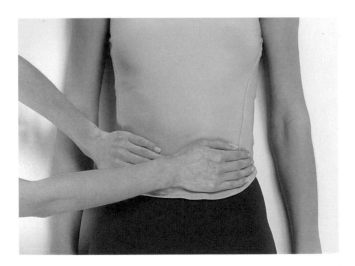

The lower abdomen

Here, the therapist places their hands in a low "V" when treating women, and in a high "V" when treating men (to avoid any contact with the genital areas). This position continues to work on the process of elimination and balancing emotions. It also regulates the sex drive and aids fertility. Regular treatment can improve hormone imbalances.

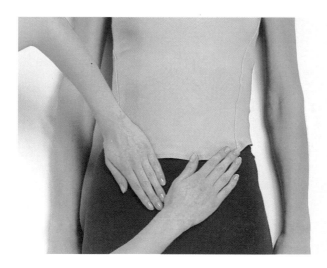

The knees

In this position the therapist places one hand on each of your knees, allowing them to bring energy down your legs to prevent it from stagnating in your body. It helps knee strain, frees the joints to increase mobility and boosts circulation in the legs. It also governs the emotion of moving forward in life. Treating the legs is essential when healing leg, ankle and foot injuries.

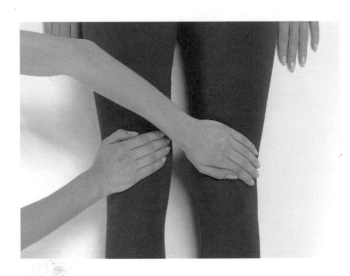

The ankles

Here, the therapist places one hand on each of your ankles. This position continues to draw energy down through your legs, helping to relieve tiredness in this area and ankle strain. It also affects the reflex points and meridian lines in the ankles that relate to the reproductive organs. Once your therapist has treated this area, they will ask you to turn over onto your front.

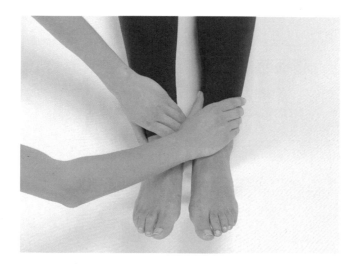

The left shoulder

In this position the therapist puts their hands over your left shoulder muscle and shoulder blade. Most people carry tension in the shoulders and upper back, which can cause both the back and head to ache. This position warms your shoulder muscles, allowing them to relax deeply and release tension. It is said that the left shoulder carries the tension of your past.

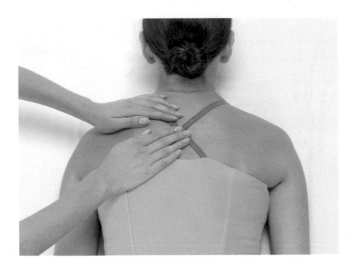

The right shoulder

In this position the therapist puts their hands over your right shoulder muscle and shoulder blade. It is said that the right shoulder carries your present tensions. Pains in the left shoulder often move to the right shoulder before completely disappearing. Emotions held in this area can also be released in this deep state of relaxation. You may find yourself crying tears of release.

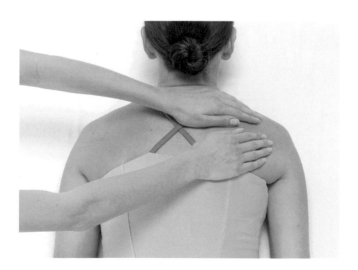

The middle of the back

In this position the therapist puts their hands one in front of the other across your back. This brings energy into your lungs and kidneys, and releases tension in your back muscles — it is usually muscle trauma and tensions that displace the vertebrae. When the muscles are relaxed with Reiki, the bones simply realign themselves naturally.

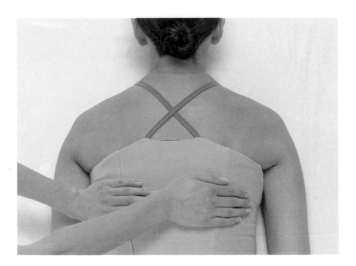

The waist

Here, the therapist puts their hands one in front of the other across your waist. A major cause of tension in this area is bad posture, which affects the lower spine area. This position relaxes the lower back by releasing any tension in the muscles. It strengthens the spine and allows energy to flow both up and down. It also aids the digestive process.

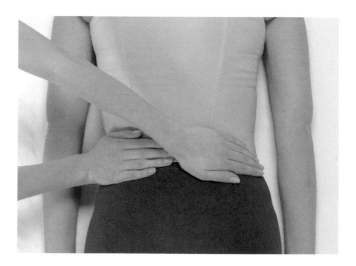

The lower back (sacrum)

Here, the therapist places their hands side by side on your lower back, over the sacrum . This releases tension in this area and increases the flow of energy down the legs. If you have a particular lower back problem it usually means that you have issues with support in your life. If the therapist holds your neck and lower back at the same time, it increases the success of the treatment.

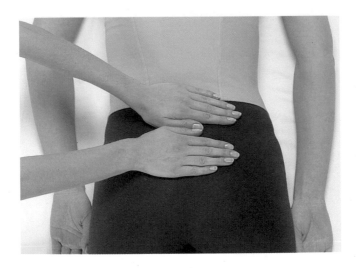

The backs of the knees

In this position the therapist places one hand in front of the other behind each of your knees. The backs of the knees are surprisingly sensitive areas and this position feeds energy into the knee tissues. Treating this area helps with varicose veins and generally boosts circulation. It also draws energy down from the torso to be grounded in the feet.

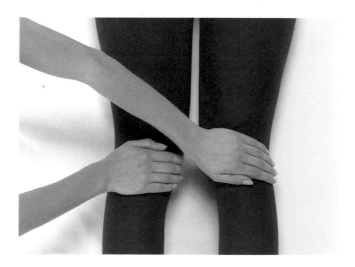

The soles of the feet

The therapist holds the soles of your feet with their palms, which feels very comforting. The rest of your body is by now deeply relaxed, yet you will still be consciously aware of the soles of your feet. This is the part of us that connects with Mother Earth and our sense of belonging. When stress causes people to feel ungrounded, this position brings them "home".

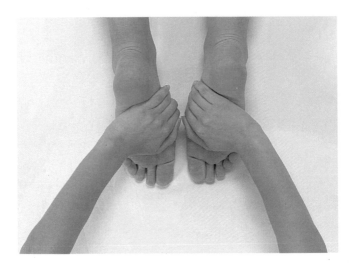

THE FINISHING-OFF TECHNIQUE

The purpose of the finishing-off technique is to gently reawaken the person from their relaxed state. It brings an energetic yet calm feeling to the body and the mind back into the present. This is especially important if the client is feeing tired or suffers from depression.

The technique consists of gently rotating the left foot to free the ankle, rubbing the toes and the sole of the foot, and squeezing up the leg three times to wake up the tissues and bring your attention back to the body. Next the therapist will flick the leg up toward the centre three times to invigorate and enliven you. This is repeated on the right leg and each of the arms in turn. Arm and joint pains are addressed by holding the hand and the upper spine, then the shoulder joint, the elbow joint and the wrist. The back is stimulated with three downward flicks either side of the spine, and the treatment finishes with a gentle rub of the back. The therapist separates their energy field from yours and gives gratitude to the Reiki. Finally, you rest for a few minutes and drink water.

The wish for healing has always been half of health.

SENECA

(4 BCE–65 AD)

Healing is a matter of time, but it is sometimes
also a matter of opportunity.

HIPPOCRATES

(460–377 BCE)

Chapter Three

learning Reiki yourself

The first step in learning Reiki yourself is to take Reiki First Degree — a two-day workshop in which you gain access to the universal energy that heals. On this course you undergo the four Reiki attunements, which are given by the Reiki Master to make it possible for you to access universal energy. You are taught how to apply a full body treatment to another person and you also experience a treatment yourself. You learn the importance of the finishing-off technique and other ways of grounding the Reiki recipient. Other integral parts of Reiki First Degree include learning how to do a self-treatment and how to heal babies, children and animals. It is not necessary to take any further training if you simply wish to practise on yourself, your family and your friends.

The unique beauty of Reiki is that once you have learned it you can treat yourself whenever and wherever the need arises. The best time to practise self-treatment is in bed at night to help to release the tensions of the day and to promote good sleep; or first thing in the morning to begin the day calm, clear-headed and energized. Some people find it helps them to relax if they give themselves Reiki when they return home from work. Reiki can be practised wherever you are – whether on the bus, in the park or even in the office.

THE FOUR ESSENTIAL REIKI ATTUNEMENTS

The attunements are performed one-to-one with the Master. They give the student access to universal energy through "tuning in" the student's electromagnetic field – rather like putting up an aerial on a radio and tuning in to a specific channel. This paticular frequency is for the purpose of healing.

The attunements are performed as a short ceremony which honours the tradition of Reiki and activates the student in such a way that the energy can come *through* them (not *from* them) for evermore. During the ceremony, the student is required to give something to the Master in exchange for the gift of Reiki – usually a course fee but it can be a donation of their skills or their time.

During the attunement several of Dr Usui's symbols are used to activate and direct the energy. The master makes an invocation in which they call upon the universal energy to align itself to the energy vortexes in the student. Usually, the student feels nothing other than deep peace and calm, but sometimes they see light or colours, or feel an intense heat emanating from their hands. Once the first attunement has been performed, the student may begin to feel the Reiki in their hands or tingling down their arms, and they may even have a fizzing sensation above their head. It is usually described as a very pleasant experience.

Each attunement is slightly different. The first focuses on the Crown chakra, the second on the Throat Chakra, the third on the Heart Chakra and the fourth on the Solar Plexus Chakra. The fourth attunement also seals the change and integrates the student's electromagnetic field for the purpose of healing.

Reiki is then ready to be applied in the form of treatment to oneself or, as described earlier, on another person. By focusing on ourselves first and foremost, we begin to take responsibility for our own well-being. Personal transformation is at hand if we are willing to abandon our bad habits and insecurities and look for wisdom and guidance. Reiki is an intelligent energy that teaches as it is practised — Reiki is the true master. The

feedback that you receive from others and indeed that you feel yourself, will open your mind and understanding to how the energy works in and around you all the time. Form follows thought – what and how you think in this moment will create what happens to you in the future. Living better with Reiki comes about through listening to the energy within and around you and beginning to create new, better ways of thinking and acting.

By focusing on the warm sensations that Reiki creates you will find comfort and peace. I suggest that you begin with a ten- to fifteen-minute self-treatment every day. Once you start to enjoy not only the physical sensations, but also the changes that begin to take place in your health and attitude, you may wish to do more.

Reiki self-treatment can be a form of meditation if you focus more consciously on the sensations that occur in each new position. By allowing your breath to slow, you can turn your attention away from your thoughts and onto the beautiful warmth pouring into your body from your own hands. As you focus on this feeling you can also reflect on the Reiki precepts (see pp.18–21).

THE EFFECTS OF LONG-TERM SELF-TREATMENT

Many people only notice the beneficial effects of long-term Reiki self-treatment when they become lazy and give up practising for a few weeks. It is only when stress begins to build up again and aches and pains start to return that they realize the true benefits of Reiki.

It may take some time for physical illnesses to respond to Reiki, but once you notice an improvement, daily self-treatment will prevent them from returning. The immediately obvious changes that take place are mental ones – clearer thinking, a greater ability to cope with emotions, better communication skills and a general return to "the old you". Your happy self can return only when you dissolve the tensions that keep you unhappy. For many of us this means starting to let your heart rather than your head guide you through life. Long-term self-treatment teaches you how to understand and tune in to the language of your heart, which many of us have long forgotten.

THE HAND POSITIONS
FOR SELF-TREATMENT

This a full-body self-treatment Reiki programme for daily use. Find a quiet place where you will not be disturbed and lie down or sit comfortably. Focus on your breath and relax. Then begin, holding each position for about two minutes.

The eyes

By holding your mind still in this position, you begin to *feel* still and turn your sense of sight inward. Focus on enjoying the quietness. Give yourself permission to do nothing for fifteen to twenty minutes while you leave the outside world behind to rest and recharge.

The top of the head

This position balances the brain, quietening mental chatter and easing agitation. Remember the Reiki precepts (see pp.18–21) and repeat them silently to yourself three times. Relax and enjoy the peace.

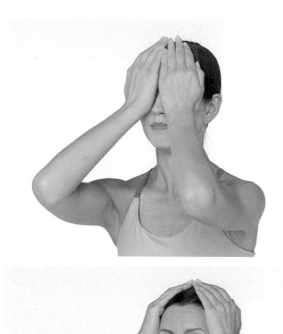

The jaws and face

In this position feel the comfort of your own touch and the sensations of heat or cold. Tell yourself that being by yourself and focusing on your well-being is the best thing that you can be doing right now.

The back of the head

As you cradle your head, release any tension in your neck – a frequent cause of headaches. If you regularly suffer from headaches, try holding one hand at the back of your head and one on your forehead. Gently comfort your mind if it struggles to keep a hold on you by commenting on your progress.

The ears

Place your hands over your ears, be quiet and still, and appreciate the sound of silence. Listen to your heartbeat as the life force gently courses through you, without you having to do anything. Notice that the silence is not truly silent as long as you can hear your heart beating. Begin to hear what is really there instead of what you want to hear. Feel your balance returning.

The throat

Release tension in the throat by breathing deeply and speaking from the voicebox. Place your hands gently around your throat to energize the glands in this area – the first line of defence against infection. Transform your anger and become more assertive and creative.

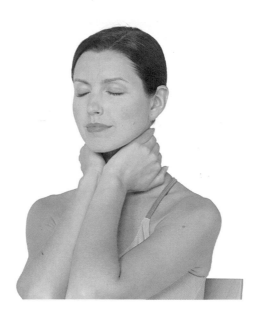

The heart and solar plexus

In this position you place one hand over your heart and the other over your solar plexus. Feel the warmth and comfort of holding your heart and relaxing your diaphragm. Breathe gently yet deeply. Release all hurt and tension and feel that you are healing any harm that has ever been done to you. Feel strong and courageous and tune in to the language of your heart.

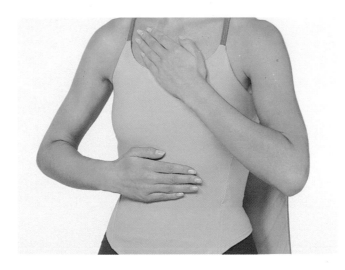

The lower abdomen

Here you gently rest your hands in a "V" on your lower abdomen, bringing comfort and aiding digestion,and elimination. This position balances the muscles of the intestinal wall and energizes the reproductive organs, which in turn balances the hormone system. It also calms emotional upsets, letting you digest what life gives you and eliminate anything of no further use.

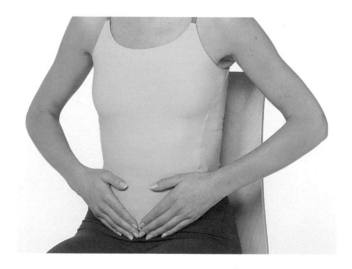

The knees

Place your hands first on your left knee and then on your right knee, with one hand on top and one underneath. Notice the energy awaken your legs and free your joints. Your path forward on life's journey will become clearer.

The ankles and feet

Place your right hand on top of your left ankle and wrap your left hand around the sole of your left foot. Then, repeat the other way around with your right foot. Feel the fabulous warmth in your feet – the feet that work so hard to keep you upright and balanced. Give them some attention and enjoy the pleasant sensation.

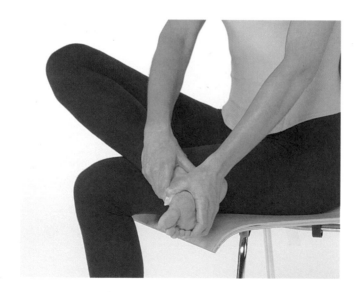

THE FINISHING-OFF TECHNIQUE FOR SELF-TREATMENT

The finishing-off technique is like an invigorating shower — awakening and stimulating. Beginning with your right foot, squeeze each of your toes in turn. Squeeze the rest of your foot firmly, including the ankle. Then, squeeze up the leg three times to bring the energy into your centre. This will help you to feel alert and grounded in the present again. Using both hands, stroke up the leg three times toward you and flick off at the end. Repeat with your left foot and leg.

Continue with your hands and arms. Squeeze each of the fingers on your right hand in turn, then the palm of the hand and the wrist. Squeeze up the arm three times toward the centre, and include the shoulder muscle where much tension is stored. Flick up the arm three times. Repeat with the left hand and arm.

Now tap the tips of your fingers all over your skull in a galloping motion. This helps to stimulate the brain and scalp and is very good before and after much thinking.

Put your hands across your chest and give gratitude for this Reiki healing. Sit still for a minute or two and notice how different you feel — how much lighter and more alive your body feels, yet relaxed and strong. Be aware of your breath and how your mind has quietened.

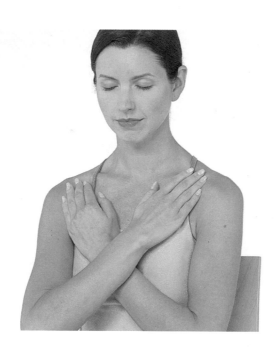

TREATING FAMILY AND FRIENDS

Reiki First Degree training will teach you not only how to do in-depth Reiki self-treatment but also how to give Reiki to your family and friends. When you have this healing ability in your own hands you no longer feel powerless when a member of your family or a friend is ill or in pain. Also, when someone is unhappy or grieving you can offer them comfort and support through a treatment, which is more effective than words could ever be.

Many people find that hectic modern lifestyles give little opportunity for quality time with loved ones, Giving and receiving Reiki is a wonderful way in which to express love between partners — learning Reiki together promotes intimacy, allowing you to help each other as well as to be close. Friendships, too, can benefit from this gift. Reiki is another vehicle for getting to know your friends better. You may be surprised at how many of them volunteer for treatment.

Reiki can be useful for people of any age and babies respond very well to it. When treating a baby it is only necessary to place the hands where you would naturally put them for a calming effect. Just hold the baby, love him or her and be still. A Reiki treatment amplifies the natural healing ability of a parent and gives them the knowledge of how to treat the whole person rather than a paticular condition. If parents focus on time-out, rest and self-treatment, their baby will feel calmer too.

As the baby grows many opportunities for comforting and healing him or her present themselves – for example, when they have colic or are teething; or when they have a bad cold or an ear infection.

Reiki is easy to practise on older children. It is not necessary for them to keep still for an hour or to lie down and receive the full session, unless they want to. Just put on their favourite video and adapt the positions to head, heart, shoulders, tummy, back and feet. It is natural for a parent to say to the child, "Show me where it hurts". By putting your warm hand on the point of discomfort and sending your child love, you will help to heal and comfort him or her. Children particularly love the finishing-off technique and may wriggle and giggle during this.

While Reiki gives parents a powerful healing tool that augments their love for their child, we should not forget that it also offers parents who share treatments with each other a special bond at a time when the little one often steals all the attention.

Older members of the family, too, can derive comfort from Reiki, especially if they live alone after having spent many years as part of a couple, or if they live in a care home. Many old people long just to be held and feel close to someone. They may need revitalizing, or they may simply feel lonely and crave human contact.

Many people also regard their pets as part of the family and Reiki can be safely used on animals. Pets tend to seek out the healing heat of your hands when they are injured or unwell. To treat your pet or any animal, simply adapt the positions and shorten the treatment. Often animals prefer to be stroked, as still hands makes them wary. It is good to focus on their head to balance their thinking process and on their heart to calm them. It may also benefit the animal to treat its spine and legs. Reiki makes pets feel secure and gives them a sense of place.

REIKI FOR PREGNANCY AND CHILDBIRTH

Reiki can be used effectively to help balance hormones and increase fertility. Also, it has been found to help women who have suffered repeated miscarriages. Most pregnant women suffer an element of anxiety and apprehension, but when you are able to give yourself a treatment, you know that you can play a significant role in your own well-being as well as that of your baby. You can improve minor ailments, such as nausea, back pain, indigestion and poor sleep. Fathers who learn Reiki can help their partners and be a part of the growing process.

During childbirth Reiki can help to ease pain and anxiety, and keep the mother focused. Research shows that women who relax during the birth require less medical intervention and stitching. Unfortunately, some babies require medical treatment or intensive care immediately after birth, which separates them from their parents. In such cases Reiki distance-healing offers the parents a way in which to remain close to their new son or daughter and to aid the healing process.

It is beautiful to do nothing — and to rest afterward.

SPANISH SAYING

Teachers open the door, but you must enter by yourself.

CHINESE PROVERB

REIKI SECOND DEGREE

Reiki Second Degree consists of a two-day course during which the student receives one further attunement. Three of the sacred symbols and mantras from Dr Usui are revealed, which act as keys to connect with subtle levels of consciousness and unlock the doorway to understanding the various forms of unseen energy. By directing the student's mind with intent, each symbol awakens a different power. The first one makes a bridge between us and a person who is absent. The second connects with their inherent mental and emotional disposition and the third sets the energy in motion. Instruction is given on how to activate these for distance-healing, in depth mental/emotional healing and the balance of situations and relationships. Anyone wishing to practise Reiki professionally must learn Reiki Second Degree. It is usually recommended that students leave a gap of six months to a year between Reiki First Degree and Reiki Second Degree, so that they can consolidate their learning and practice.

Many people live away from their family or friends. In this case, it is invaluable to learn Reiki Second Degree as it gives them the tools to be able to harness the universal energy, to direct it to whoever needs it and to activate it for complete physical, mental and emotional healing, no matter how far away the person may be. Recipients of distance-healing often report that they felt the healing at the exact time it was activated.

Children and animals may also be successfully treated at a distance, perhaps when they are asleep. In this way, they can receive the full benefit of Reiki without becoming bored with the process. However, touch is always my preference because when both parties are present a conscious connection is made from the link between the giver and the recipient.

Distance-healing has many uses. For example, when someone you love is travelling, you can send them protection for their journey. You can make a connection with them and send them love. Or if someone is in hospital you can send them healing and support when you may otherwise feel helpless.

Reiki can also be applied in this way to all aspects of your life, including situations where you may feel apprehensive, worried or overburdened, such as driving tests, job interviews or moving house. It can be used to improve relationships within the family or even at work. And when you feel more at ease with your relationships in general, your inner confidence radiates outward, subtly affecting everyone with whom you come into contact in a positive way, as well as the wider community.

Once you have achieved Reiki Second Degree, you may notice that you become calmer and gain clarity of mind. These, in turn, will help you to feel empowered and less out of control. With such empowerment, you will find that not only do you yourself begin to change for the better, but so, too, do your family and the people around you. By becoming balanced and mentally stronger you demonstrate these qualities to your family. Your children will gain an innate understanding of living a balanced life without you having to teach them. Reiki puts you in the driving seat so that you can make plans, aim high and watch a new, better life unfold before you.

So divinely is the world organized that every one
of us, in our place and time, is in balance with
everything else.

WOLFGANG VON GOETHE

(1749–1832)

The best and safest thing is to keep a balance in
your life, acknowledge the great powers around us
and in us. If you can do that, and live that way,
you are really a wise man.

EURIPIDES

(484–406 BCE)

Chapter Four

the nature of being

When we receive our Reiki attunements, the Master opens up a gateway through which we are able to access the universal life force. This enables us to heal ourselves (and others) and to begin the process of integrating our mind, body, spirit and emotions to become whole again.

Once the healing process is underway, many Reiki students experience a reawakening of consciousness, as they are able – albeit fleetingly at first – to connect with the Divine and glimpse their own true nature. This can cause them to feel dissatisfaction with everyday life, until they realize that through continued Reiki practice they are making a gradual yet fundamental shift from focusing on "doing" to focusing on "being". Through the simple act of laying our hands on ourselves with compassion we are able to turn inward, away from our senses and reach an inner sanctum of blissful expanded consciousness. And the more we practise Reiki, the easier it becomes to reach this state – until we become so familiar with it that it becomes our usual state of being.

In this chapter we explore ways in which we can integrate our bodies, minds, emotions and souls to aid Reiki healing, through tools such as meditation and making lifestyle changes. We also look at further Reiki training, from practitioner to Master levels.

HEALING THE BODY

The body is a physical fusion of spirit, emotion and mind, combined with experience and habit. How we think of ourselves is largely our own perception of who we are, added to the basis provided by our heritage and coloured with the knowledge we have gathered so far in our lives. In other words, our past creates our present, which in turn determines our future.

It follows, then, that the way we treat our body today will have a considerable impact on our health in the future. Our physical traits are passed down in our genetic makeup but that doesn't mean that we cannot improve our well-being by becoming more health-conscious in our behaviour and actions.

The first, all-important step toward healing your body is to place your hands on it in a kind and loving way, and wish it well. Then, by receiving Reiki, or better still, by giving yourself Reiki on an ongoing basis, you can begin the healing process to restore your body to optimum health and enjoy a happier, more fulfilling life.

CHANGING THE DIALOGUE OF THE MIND

Through the gentle reawakening that happens with continued Reiki practice, daily life becomes more balanced. You no longer feel at the mercy of the world, and your own mind is more in control of the planning and the shaping of your own destiny – as you think, so it shall become.

The mind is a condensation of the emotions, which is in a constant state of flux. In India the analogy used to describe the nature of the mind is that of a monkey that jumps from branch to branch high up in a tree. The monkey needs to be disciplined and trained so that it can rest and be calm. You can try to restrain it, but when it breaks free again it will not be happy. Far better, then, to befriend it and guide it under your tutelage. We train our monkey-mind through reminding it how to be still: we can contemplate, we can learn to meditate, we can become conscious of our breath and slow ourselves down and we can use our own hands to hold ourselves still. The monkey-mind has forgotten what bliss there is in silence, for rarely does it cease for a moment. Indeed even in our sleep it still chatters on and randomly frolics in the trees. No wonder we often awaken in the morning more tired than when we went to bed.

When the mind is agitated there is corresponding agitation in the body; when there is tension and agitation in the body, there is corresponding agitation in the mind. So, only when body and mind both settle down can our emotions begin to feel free.

It generally takes many years of daily practice to gain real mastery over the mind. However, in the meantime we can change the content of our minds so that it benefits our growth, rather than sabotages our progress. In order to be able to do this, it is necessary to quieten mental chatter to a point where we can consciously implant affirmations in the mind.

Affirmations, as we have seen in Chapter 1 (see pp.18–21), are positive statements. To write your own affirmation, firstly write down the negative thoughts and feelings that you have regularly. Notice the way you comment and judge both the world around you and your own self. What do you feel you cannot do? Why do you feel you cannot do these things? For example: "I am stressed and unwell because I am overwhelmed with all the things I have to do". "I am afraid to leave my current job as I feel I won't be able to cope with a new one" and even "I'm too fat/ugly/old/stupid for anyone to love me", or "When I look to the future I am afraid of the emptiness".

Now write down, using the present tense and the first person, how you would like to think and feel. Your affirmation could be along the lines of: "I am healthy, happy and good at prioritising what I need to do." "I welcome change and look forward to the challenge of something new", "I am able to love and be loved because I am at ease with myself" or "When I look to the future I see great potential and lots of possibilities."

Spend a little time being still each day. Good times to do this are first thing in the morning when you get up or just before you go to bed at night. Practise Reiki self-treatment, if you have been taught; if not, simply cup your eyes as in the first position for self-treatment (see pp.74–5), and then adopt the heart and solar plexus position (see p.80). These two positions will begin to give you a sense of peace and create fertile ground in which to plant your affirmation.

Next, reflect on your affirmation. Say it out loud three times and *mean* it. Say it in your head three times and *mean* it. Say it with true conviction, as if you really want the affirmation to become reality. Tell yourself that if other people can feel this way, then so can you. Those other people feel this way because they have tamed their monkey-mind and taught it to be on their side. So, whenever you catch yourself feeling or thinking negatively, bring your attention back to your affirmation and think positively. If your mind resists change, say the affirmation out loud to reinforce the message.

Try to keep your affirmation at the back of your mind at all times, so that you are constantly aware of it, its meaning and its implications. You could even write it down several times on pieces of paper and stick them in prominent places at home and at work, such as on your dressing table or on your computer, to remind yourself to focus on it.

It is not only for what we do that we are held
responsible, but also for what we do not do.

MOLIÈRE

(1622-73)

You must be the change you wish to see in the world.

MAHATMA GANDHI

(1869-1948)

THE EMOTIONS

Our bodies consist of a combination of different ener-
gies – from our emotions, our minds and our souls. The
emotions are a natural, instinctive reaction to stimuli
from the outside world. Everybody has them. You may
not be able to see the emotions themselves, yet you can
see their consequences as you respond physically to
them. In this way, our past emotional reactions to people, places and experiences create a behavioural pattern
that determines or contributes to our present feelings.

Our emotions are the barometer with which we gauge
our own truth. It is only when our emotional self is
healed that we become whole. We can take care of our
bodies and discipline our minds, but it is in the realm of
emotion that our metamorphosis begins. The emotions
connect with the soul through the heart . If you were to
listen to your heart instead of your mind, your life would
improve dramatically because you would bring more
love into your world. The emotions are a bridge to the
soul as they fuse spirit with mind and body.

THE SOUL

Many of us experience dissatisfaction with our lives – a deep longing for something that seems to elude us constantly. Although the materialistic world in which we live might try to make us believe otherwise, that missing part of us is our soul.

The soul is infinite, yet it is personal. It is you. Your soul is different from my soul. Yet the soul is in union with the Divine, and through this we are one. It is via the soul that we can experience unity with our creative energy – the universal life force – that makes and sustains all things. Your soul is the gateway to experiencing the Divine within you.

The soul has no boundaries, yet you recognize it when it reveals itself to you. It is only in stillness and silence that this revelation can occur. Then, gradually, by frequently reconnecting with your soul through Reiki practice, it becomes more and more familiar until you are aware of its presence at all times. In truth, your soul was always there, you were simply unaware of it.

REASSESSING HABITS AND LIFESTYLES

When you practise Reiki regularly you may find yourself constantly reassessing your life on many different levels. This is a good time to make a determined effort to understand yourself more fully, so that you can make positive changes.

A good place to start is by writing down your thoughts and feelings about your lifestyle. Make a list of all the things you would be better off without. For example, ask yourself if there are any habits that you would like to give up if only you had the willpower or knowledge how to? Have you often promised yourself that you would stop smoking, or give up alcohol or chocolate, but then constantly put off the day of reckoning? Do you eat a healthy, balanced diet or do you have lots of processed meals and refined fatty foods? Is your home as neat and tidy as you'd like or is it cluttered and chaotic? Do you have a tendency to get depressed and look on the down-side of everything? Or do you work too hard so that you are overtired and irritable? and so on.

Now, instead of what you *shouldn't* do, begin to look at what you *can* do to improve your life positively and actively. For example, if you are overweight, join a slimming club and take some exercise. Or if you want to be physically healthier, drink more water, eat more vegetables or go for a walk every day. You could spend more time with your partner, children, parents or friends; you could take up a hobby or sport; or you could give yourself some quality "me-time" in which to do something you really love doing.

You can use Reiki self-treatment to help you make changes. For example, if you are a smoker, lie down and practise the eye position (pp.74–5), followed by the heart and solar plexus position (p.80), when you have the urge. Create an affirmation to help you give up and pledge to save the money you spend on cigarettes for a holiday instead. If you feel depressed or overtired, practise the finishing-off technique (pp.84–5) three times in a row first thing each the morning. Then create an affirmation, such as "I am happy and full of energy". As you practise self-treatment regularly, you will begin to

feel better physically, mentally and emotionally because Reiki rebalances energy and restores well-being.

From time to time most people's lives stagnate. At such times one of the most helpful and productive activities can be clutter-busting or sorting through the piles of "stuff" that we accumulate. This requires discipline to be successful. Make a rule that you will tidy away anything that you cannot do without; and give anything that you no longer need or want to a charity shop, or throw it away. Clearing clutter shifts energy. Giving things away creates space to be filled. Make it space filled with peace and creativity rather than with "stuff".

Once you have decided which changes you wish to make, don't try to change everything at once. Instead, introduce them gradually. Don't expect to see results overnight, but if you make positive affirmations about your intentions, you may be surprised at how quickly things improve. The result will be better health and general well-being. As your life becomes more balanced, you will have more time for yourself, gain renewed self-esteem and rediscover what happiness really means.

MEDITATION AND BREATH

Breathing is an involuntary action – we do it without thinking. However, the way in which we breathe affects our well-being, just as our states of health and mind affect how we breathe. For example, rapid, shallow breathing makes us feel anxious and stressed, whereas slow, deep breathing calms and relaxes us. Likewise, when we are anxious or stressed our breathing becomes fast and shallow, whereas when we are content and relaxed our breathing is slower and deeper. By learning how to control our breathing voluntarily we can benefit greatly both physically and mentally. One of the best ways in which to do this is through meditation.

As we have seen in Chapter 1 (see pp.18–21), Reiki can be used as a focus for meditation. Find somewhere quiet and peaceful, lie down and close your eyes. Place your hands in the heart and solar plexus position, turn your attention inward, away from the senses and focus on your breath. Then, reflect on the act of breathing itself. Consider how we always take one breath in, followed by one breath out. That is the natural order of things – the two actions follow each other and are mutually exclusive because it is impossible to do them both at the same time.

Now monitor *how* you are breathing. Watch your breath as it goes from an in-breath to an out-breath, and back to an in-breath again. Notice that there is a point between each changeover when the breath is still for a moment. To help you to focus, in your mind say to yourself "re" as you inhale, and "lax" as you exhale. On "re" your body takes in oxygen to nourish itself, drawing strength and vitality from the air. On "lax" your body releases tension, as it expels carbon dioxide.

Now, imagine yourself filling with light and energy as you inhale – breathe in love. As you exhale imagine the foggy smoke of unwanted thoughts and habits gently leaving. Let them go because you no longer need them – breathe out fear.

End the meditation by focusing once more on the act of breathing for a couple of minutes. Then, slowly sit up, open your eyes again and readjust yourself to the world.

MEDITATION IN ACTION

If you find meditating while lying down difficult, you might like to try this "action" meditation instead.

Find a quiet place outside, preferably somewhere with grass, and start walking in a large circle. Look down in front of you but don't focus on anything in particular. Gradually slow down your pace until you reach the point at which you begin to wobble and feel unbalanced. Now speed up just a little until you are walking as slow as you can *without* wobbling. Continue to walk slowly and practise the "re" and "lax" breathing, together with the inhalation of vitality and the exhalation of unwanted thoughts and habits (see p.115). Notice the sensations in your hands. Are they warm? Do they tingle? Do the sensations seem to increase the longer you walk in this way? If possible, practise this meditation with a like-minded friend or family member, because in the company of another person the experience is more intense and your staying power is increased. Use this meditation whenever you feel a need to replenish yourself.

REIKI WITH OTHER THERAPIES

Normally I recommend that you have Reiki on its own because it is one of the simplest, yet most effective and complete treatments you can receive. However, I acknowledge that it is sometimes beneficial for a client to have several different therapies in one session. For example, a therapist may give a massage or a reflexology treatment and then bring in Reiki whenever they feel the need or if there seems to be an energy block. Often practitioners use Reiki at the end of another type of treatment, such as acupuncture or chiropractic, to integrate the changes that have taken place and to prevent the client from possibly suffering a strong or uncomfortable reaction.

Reiki can be used in combination with any complementary therapy that works by rebalancing the body's energy system, from acupuncture, homeopathy, reflexology and aromatherapy to chiropractic, the Bowen Technique, the Alexander Technique, Indian head massage and Emotional Therapy.

Reiki is also the perfect complement to conventional medical treatment. I have taught Reiki to many doctors, who mostly learn it for their own stress management as they feel it is inappropriate to take on the role of hands-on healer. Yet many doctors recommend their patients either to receive Reiki treatments or, preferably, to learn Reiki themselves. In this way, the patient becomes less dependent on drug therapy and starts to take responsibility for their own health.

In addition, Reiki is a useful tool for any therapist who needs to replenish their own energy between clients. For example, a busy masseur might find it draining to give six or seven massages in one day and could use Reiki self-treatment to help them to regain their strength. Reiki can also help therapists to deal with any unwelcome emotional issues which are triggered by issues with and reactions from clients. I strongly recommend that, as a matter of course, therapists spend fifteen to twenty minutes at the end of each working day giving themselves Reiki to rebalance their vitality and dissipate any negative residue left by their work.

TAKING REIKI FURTHER

Some Reiki Masters allow their students to practise as therapists as soon as they have completed their first course. However, I prefer to train my therapists to a high professional standard that not only protects the client and gives them the quality of treatment and support they need, but also ensures that the therapists are properly prepared to deal with clients. The standards I adhere to are also set as training criteria by the British-based International Guild of Professional Practitioners.

To become a Reiki practitioner you need to have taken First and Second Degree courses. However, becoming a therapist is not merely a matter of learning the Reiki technique and then offering it to people for a fee. Many would-be therapists find it invaluable to take a special course that covers practice management and communication skills. On this course you learn how to manage your practice, whether you work from home or in a clinic. You learn how to: listen properly, empathize, refer a client on to someone else and communicate effectively. You are also taught about equipment, the therapeutic environment, insurance, ethics and codes of conduct, book-keeping and client record-keeping. In addition, you need to study basic anatomy and physiology, gain a first-aid certificate and be closely mentored in the early stages of working with clients.

You need to leave a gap of at least one year after completing Reiki Second Degree before you can undertake Master's Level 1. It is a personal mastery course that offers attunement into Divine light and reveals the Master's mantra and symbol. You learn a sonic meditation technique to enhance the dissipation of negativity and increase awareness of the present. The seed of light is planted in your heart and awareness begins to grow from the inside. This level is ideal for those who wish to go deeper into Reiki without teaching.

The Master's Degree Level 2 is an apprenticeship of three years, by invitation only, for practitioners with at least three years' professional experience. It instructs the student in all aspects of teaching and includes a teacher-training qualification.

Come away all by yourself to some lonely
place and rest for a while.

JESUS

MARK 6:31

We shall find peace. We shall hear the angels,
we shall see the sky sparkling with diamonds.

CHEKHOV

(1860-1904)

CONCLUSION

Through continued Reiki treatment or practice you will find your true self and discover meaning in your life. When this happens well-being becomes your natural state of health. And once your tensions, aches and illnesses are banished, you will gain a new clarity of vision about your personal destiny. You can only gain insight into the purpose of your life when you are clear of clutter in body, mind and feelings. When all these aspects become integrated, you remember what it is to listen to your heart, rather than your head.

The heart is the gateway to the soul. If our vision becomes clear enough to let us understand intuitively the language of our heart, our soul can once again play its intended role in our daily life. Then, if we are lucky, instead of being something we randomly connect with, our soul becomes a familiar companion that leads us through life with wisdom and guidance. The voice of the soul is the voice of truth. It is reached via the heart, through the pathway of our feelings.

How do we attain the necessary clarity to be able to access our hearts and souls once more? We must aim to tame and balance our minds, in order to purify our feelings. We must strengthen our bodies with a healthy diet, by drinking more water, taking fresh air and exercise and by showing our bodies respect. Remember that your body is the vehicle for the invisible aspects of your self. As you awaken and discover a new sense of wellness, happiness returns as your natural state of being.

When we continue practising Reiki, our personality gradually changes too. Through ongoing healing and treatment, our inner child learns to ignore the outside world and turns inward to listen to our own innate truth and to live in the present moment. Being able to live in the moment is a gift, that is why it is called "the present". Enjoy the present and take care of the gift. Know that everything you need to reach your true potential is already inside you. By holding yourself still in a place of calm through your Reiki practice you will come to see with clarity. By seeing you will come to know, and by knowing you will come to enjoy your life to the full.

INDEX

Picture Credits

The publisher would like to thank the following people and photographic libraries for permission to reproduce their material. Every care has been taken to trace copyright holders. However, if we have omitted anyone we apologise and will, if informed, make corrections in any future editions.

Page 1 Getty Images/Taxi/Miguel S Salmeron; **16** Getty Images/ Stone/Art Wolfe; **23** Getty Images/Stone/Art Wolfe; **33** Getty Images/Taxi/Miguel S Salmeron; **39** Getty Images/Stone/Robert Daly; **64** Getty Images/Stone/Sara Gray; **70** Rubberball Productions; **73** Getty Images/Stone/George Hunter; **91** Rubberball Productions; **94** Photolibrary.com/Jessica Hromas; **97** Getty Images/Image Bank/Robert Holmgren; **101** Getty Images/Stone/David Roth; **107** Getty Images/Image Bank/Dennie Cody; **112** ZEFA/Miles; **117** Getty Images/Stone/Victoria Pearson; **122** ImageDJ

Author's Acknowledgments

Thanks to Tim and Penny Prince for everything; to Kim and Taz for being; to Sue Kay and Carolyn Finlay for inspiration; and to all of them for their love.

Publisher's Acknowledgments

Models: Caroline Long and Suzi Langhorne
Make-up artist: Tinks Reding